GRAPHIC EXPEDITIONS

# Rescue in ANTARCTICA

AN *Isabel Soto* GEOGRAPHY ADVENTURE

by Emily Sohn

illustrated by Steven Butler and Anne Timmons

Consultant:
Christina Hulbe
Associate Professor, Department of Geology
Portland State University
Portland, Oregon

Capstone
press

Mankato, Minnesota

Graphic Library is published by Capstone Press,
151 Good Counsel Drive, P.O. Box 669, Mankato, Minnesota 56002.
www.capstonepub.com

062010
005833R

*Library of Congress Cataloging-in-Publication Data*
Sohn, Emily.
    Rescue in Antarctica: an Isabel Soto geography adventure / by Emily Sohn;
        illustrated by Steven Butler and Anne Timmons.
    p. cm. — (Graphic library. Graphic expeditions)
    Summary: "In graphic novel format, follows the adventures of Isabel Soto as she
leads a rescue mission in Antarctica" — Provided by publisher.
    Includes bibliographical references and index.
    ISBN 978-1-4296-3408-3 (library binding)
    ISBN 978-1-4296-3896-8 (paperback)
    1. Antarctica — Description and travel — Comic books, strips, etc. — Juvenile
literature. 2. Search and rescue operations — Antarctica — Comic books, strips, etc. —
Juvenile literature. 3. Graphic novels. I. Butler, Steven, ill. II. Timmons, Anne, ill. III. Title.
IV. Series.
G863.S645 2010
919.8'9 — dc22
                                                                                2009005052

*Designer*
Alison Thiele

*Cover Artist*
Tod G. Smith

*Colorist*
Krista Ward

*Media Researcher*
Wanda Winch

*Editor*
Aaron Sautter

**Photo credits:** DigitalVision (Getty Images), 7; Getty Images Inc./Riser/Paul Souders, 23

**Design elements:** Shutterstock/Chen Ping Hung (framed edge design); mmmm (world
map design); Mushakesa (abstract lines design); Najin (old parchment design)

# TABLE OF CONTENTS

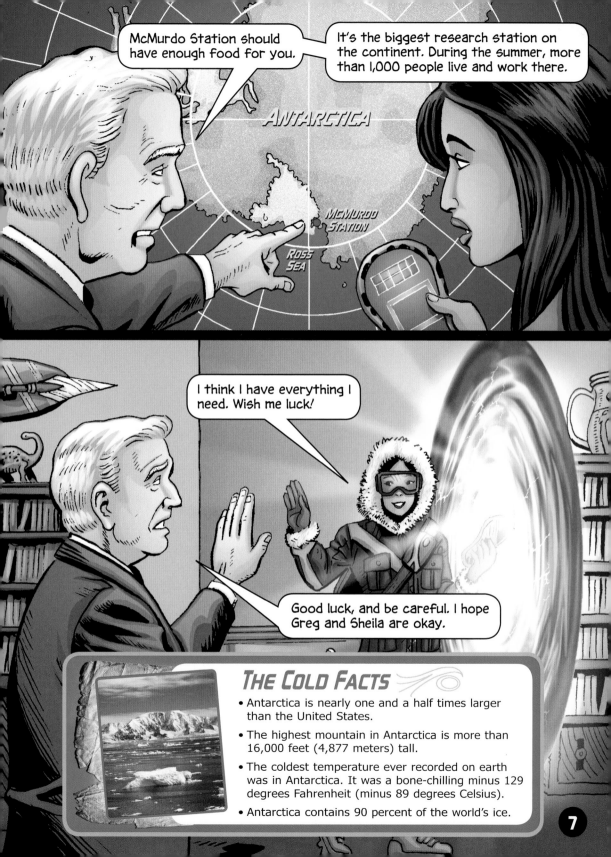

### THE COLD FACTS

- Antarctica is nearly one and a half times larger than the United States.
- The highest mountain in Antarctica is more than 16,000 feet (4,877 meters) tall.
- The coldest temperature ever recorded on earth was in Antarctica. It was a bone-chilling minus 129 degrees Fahrenheit (minus 89 degrees Celsius).
- Antarctica contains 90 percent of the world's ice.

Welcome to Antarctica, Isabel. I'm Dave, one of the glaciologists here at McMurdo Station.

Antarctica is certainly a beautiful place. But it's the driest, windiest, and coldest continent on earth.

Luckily, we have heated buildings and hot tea.

Sounds like a perfect way to warm up before heading out on our mission.

On December 5, 1914, British explorer Ernest Shackleton and his crew sailed toward Antarctica on the *Endurance*. Shackleton wanted to be the first person to cross Antarctica on foot.

But the *Endurance* never made it to land. In the Weddell Sea, the ship got stuck in the ice. On November 21, 1915, the *Endurance* was crushed by sea ice and sank.

Shackleton and his crew managed to save three small lifeboats. But the sea was frozen. They had to drag the boats across the ice. After a few days, they had only traveled a few miles. They decided to set up a camp and wait for the ice to break apart.

On April 9, 1916, the ice broke, allowing the crew to row the boats. Eventually, they made it to Elephant Island. But there was no hope for rescue. Luckily, the crew had enough supplies to set up a survival camp.

Shackleton soon made a risky decision. On April 24, 1916, he took five men and sailed a lifeboat hundreds of miles to South Georgia Island. The journey took 17 days.

The small group then hiked more than 20 miles, or 32 kilometers, over the mountains to the other side of the island. They finally found help at a whaling station.

That summer, Shackleton made three attempts to rescue his crew. But the ships had to turn back each time. Finally, on August 30, 1916, the *Yelcho* arrived at Elephant Island.

Shackleton's men were finally saved. They had spent 22 long months at sea. But they all lived to tell of their adventures.

21

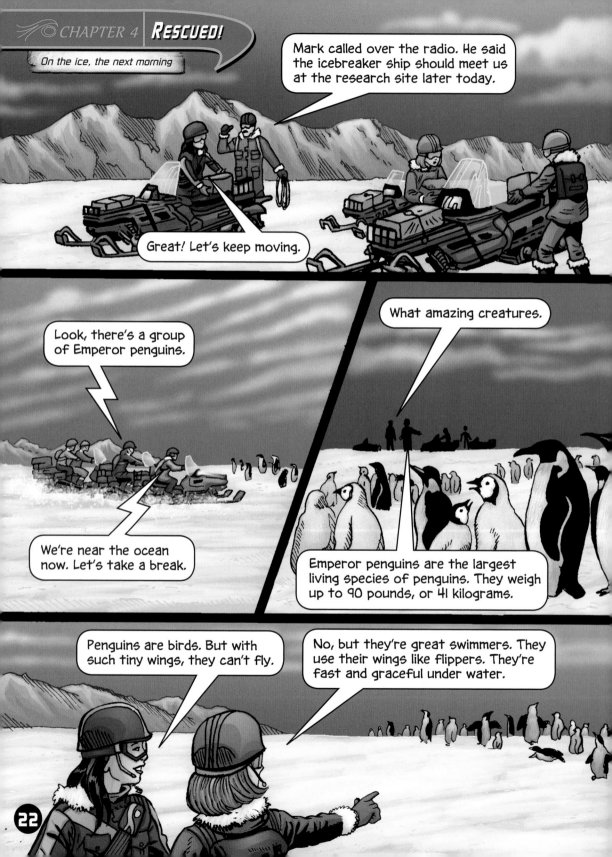

**FOR THE BABIES**

After laying an egg, female Emperor penguins travel up to 50 miles (80 kilometers) to find food in open water. While the mothers are gone, the fathers protect the eggs. They keep the eggs warm by holding them on their feet until the chicks hatch. The fathers don't eat until the mothers return about two months later.

People have long believed there was a huge continent at the southern part of the earth. Hundreds of years ago, people called it Terra Australis.

Captain James Cook tried to find Antarctica in 1773 and again in 1774. Cook and his crew were the first sailors to cross the Antarctic Circle. He came within 75 miles (121 kilometers) of Antarctica, but he never saw land. Edward Bransfield finally discovered the main Antarctic continent on January 30, 1820.

Norwegian explorer Roald Amundsen became the first explorer to reach the South Pole on December 14, 1911.

Due to the tilt of Earth's axis, Antarctica receives 24 hours of sunlight each day during the summer. The sun never completely sets. The sun does not rise during the winter months. It is dark 24 hours a day.

The average temperature at South Pole Station is minus 56 degrees Fahrenheit (minus 49 degrees Celcius). Summer temperatures at McMurdo Station can be as warm as 50 degrees Fahrenheit (10 degrees Celcius).

Emperor penguins can dive more than 700 feet (213 meters) deep. They can stay under water for nearly 20 minutes.

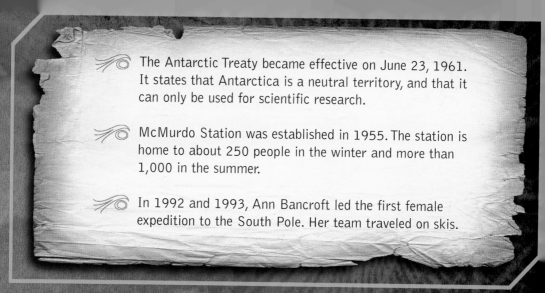

- The Antarctic Treaty became effective on June 23, 1961. It states that Antarctica is a neutral territory, and that it can only be used for scientific research.

- McMurdo Station was established in 1955. The station is home to about 250 people in the winter and more than 1,000 in the summer.

- In 1992 and 1993, Ann Bancroft led the first female expedition to the South Pole. Her team traveled on skis.

## MORE ABOUT

*Isabel Soto*

**NAME:** Dr. Isabel "Izzy" Soto
**DEGREES:** History and Anthropology
**BUILD:** Athletic   **HAIR:** Dark Brown
**EYES:** Brown   **HEIGHT:** 5' 7"

**W.I.S.P.:** The Worldwide Inter-dimensional Space/Time Portal developed by Max Axiom at Axiom Laboratory.

**BACKSTORY:** Dr. Isabel "Izzy" Soto caught the history bug as a little girl. Every night, her grandfather told her about his adventures exploring ancient ruins in South America. He believed lost cultures teach people a great deal about history.

Izzy's love of cultures followed her to college. She studied history and anthropology. On a research trip to Thailand, she discovered an ancient stone with mysterious energy. Izzy took the stone to Super Scientist Max Axiom, who determined that the stone's energy cuts across space and time. Harnessing the power of the stone, he built a device called the W.I.S.P. It opens windows to any place and any time. Izzy now travels through time to see history unfold before her eyes. Although she must not change history, she can observe and investigate historical events.

algae (AL-jee) — small plants without roots or stems that grow in water or on damp surfaces

continent (KAHN-tuh-nuhnt) — one of earth's seven large land masses

crampon (KRAM-pahn) — a metal frame with pointed metal teeth that attaches to a climber's boot; crampons give climbers secure footing on snow and ice.

crevasse (kri-VAS) — a deep, wide crack in a glacier or ice sheet

current (KUHR-uhnt) — the movement of water in a river or an ocean

fossil fuels (FAH-suhl FYOOLZ) — natural fuels formed from the remains of plants and animals; coal, oil, and natural gas are fossil fuels.

glacier (GLAY-shur) — a huge moving body of ice found in mountain valleys or polar regions

glaciologist (glay-shee-OL-uh-jist) — a scientist who studies glaciers

iceberg (EYESS-berg) — a huge piece of ice that floats in the ocean; icebergs break off from glaciers and ice sheets.

lichen (LYE-ken) — a flat, mosslike plant that grows on trees and rocks

oceanographer (oh-shuh-NOG-ruh-fer) — a scientist who studies the ocean and ocean life

SOS (ESS OH ESS) — a signal sent out to call for urgent help

terrain (tuh-RAYN) — the surface of the land

# READ MORE

Aspen-Baxter, Linda. *Antarctica.* Continents. New York: Weigl Publishers, 2006.

Binns, Tristan Boyer. *Antarctica.* Exploring Continents. Chicago: Heinemann Library, 2006.

Bledsoe, Lucy Jane. *How to Survive in Antarctica.* New York: Holiday House, 2006.

Hoena, B. A. *Shackleton and the Lost Antarctic Expedition.* Disasters in History. Mankato, Minn.: Capstone Press, 2006.

Markle, Sandra. *Animals Robert Scott Saw: An Adventure in Antarctica.* San Francisco: Chronicle Books, 2008.

# INTERNET SITES

FactHound offers a safe, fun way to find Internet sites related to this book. All of the sites on FactHound have been researched by our staff.

Here's all you do:

Visit *www.facthound.com*

FactHound will fetch the best sites for you!

# INDEX